Unendurable Illumination

Jay Passer

Copyright© 2020 Jay Passer
ISBN: 978-93-89690-53-8

First Edition: 2020
Rs. 200/-

Cyberwit.net
HIG 45 Kaushambi Kunj, Kalindipuram
Allahabad - 211011 (U.P.) India
http://www.cyberwit.net
Tel: +(91) 9415091004 +(91) (532) 2552257
E-mail: info@cyberwit.net

No part of this book may be reproduced or transmitted in any form or by
any means, electronic, mechanical, photocopying, or otherwise, without
the express written consent of Jay Passer.

Printed at Repro India Limited.

Grateful acknowledgment to the editors of the publications where some of these poems first appeared: *Durable Goods Microzine, Guerrilla Pamphlets, Horror Sleaze Trash, Philosophical Idiot, Poetry Super Highway, The Daily Dope Fiend, Unlikely Stories Mark V,* and *Your One Phone Call*

Contents

THE KISS

Surrounded in the small room
By books and boozy memory
I think of her delicate hand in mine
As we skipped down the stairs to the Powell station
So naturally enveloped in familiarity and fruition
I'd only kissed her once
On the cheek at the Tempest at 5 pm that afternoon
After the exhibit of Beat photography at the Jewish
Our thighs just touching with a hint of electrical restraint
Talking of American cities, art theory, and the history of elephants
Talking of conservation, vegetarianism, jazz singers and old standards
Just a girl I thought just a young woman
I really ought not to preconceive the seduction of this vision
A further museum visit promised and my brain fairly dancing
Her skin her eyes her angelically molded cadence of being
Resolved to court her to the end of time
I kissed her after a spontaneously parting embrace
Boldly on the lips before she disappeared past the turnstile
I could sense her invisible smile

Even though she'd earlier insisted
'This isn't exactly a date'

NOTE TO MOTHERS EVERYWHERE

have we left the womb?
in an official sense

are we still apologizing
for breaking the 2nd law of thermodynamics?
on a daily basis

try glueing that dinner plate back together
it was made from 100% high-fire media rhetoric

luckily I polished off that filet mignon
(grilled rare verging on bloody)
before high-ranking vegetarians targeted me as a terrorist

luckily we've mastered space travel
I never could find a decent parking spot

I was incubated in an oven constructed of meat and bones
and now they expect me to say thank you very much
it's great to be here?

I don't exactly remember asking for the miraculous

THE TATTOO

I got a school bus tattooed to my arm.
it will take me to that hallowed place
off the track someday.

my nephew drew the picture.
I took it to the tattoo shop
and the guy said

nice.
then he dug in like they
do.

it cost $90
plus a $50 tip.
you best pay up when someone scars you for life.

PROMISES PROMISES

weaknesses are just mistrust
of discovery.

how painful it is
when we're late for the flight,
defying destinations;

fists and martyrs
in collision.

dirty dogfights over defected territory;
that's us, maddened creatures

scrapping over food, forces, feces, fatigue;
scrapping over fodder.

all the wars combined,
wars intimate, infinite,
wars monstrously over-budget.

with jaws wired shut
how can I shout

WHY? WTF?!!!
how can I scream

as fear of mortality conquers the self
the match is lit beneath determined combustibles,

whining, winless,
wingless.

LACKING NEW PUSSY

once I rode the rails
now all I need is a garden salad

POOR RESUME

I once quit a
job
just because
I got tired of sitting
on the bus,
of seeing
the same faces
over and over again
propped up on
the same bodies
every damn
morning.

then again,
I could have just
picked
that other job
as a monk
or a bank robber
or emigrated
to wherever
they assassinate poets
for grumbling
about
routine.

I DON'T

wear white socks
drop bombs on anyone
walk on water
order the execution of my brothers or uncles
drink milk
shave very often
question the inexorable corruption of the police
admit my addiction to cinema
know a hell hole of a lot
eat okra or nopales (that shit is slimy af)

SEARCHING POCKETS FOR DINOSAUR BONES

I'll miss rain
coming down on the windowpane.

while the guy across the hall
fantasizes, penning the modern equivalent
of *The Old Man and the Sea*

I got some ice from the lobby,
and learned a word or two in Spanish from the maid.

in my future android physique
I'll miss
cracking my knuckles,

and the quick morning patter of rain,
the taste of blood on a split lip.

I frisk my government for leadership qualities,
just a paper cut short of the shredder.

it helps if you're besties
with a superhero, or a vampire.

getting by in the city today?
maybe it's best you learn to identify species of edible
fungus, grubs and tree bark.

SINCE I'VE BEEN HIDING

an elliptical
scorpion
or the trident

of your tongue

mushroom-cloud
against the
new moon

Medusa

I've grown
so tired
of dreaming

SHOPPING FOR PAINT

The money on the table was for
apples and some aspirin, not

for vodka, you dumb ass.

Nice to see you too. Why isn't there
any ice left?

Because I used it to stop up the

hole in the bathtub, and to
water the bamboo shoots.

Did you save any for
brush fires, for inevitable atomic
detonation?

What we needed was a shelter, like they got
buried underground,
in Israel.

I measured the room instead.
12' x 12' x 9'

sunlight excluded.

You! you're such a goddamned
perfectionist.

PARIS

flew to de Gaulle
came home with a nice new pair of black suede Puma kicks
since the Parisian rain destroyed my
no-name Chinatown black canvas kung-fu slip-ons

had a Perceval chef's knife shipped back to SF
(I've bought used cars for less)
which was almost lost through Customs

purchased a postcard from the Rodin Museum
of a young and terrifyingly radiant
Camille Claudel
who was institutionalized by the double-team of
her spiteful mother
and jealous brother

for the final 30 years of her life

VIRGO IN THE HOUSE

recaps all the disposable pens
dusts in all the unreachable places
employing stepladder, feather duster and
a subtle flick of the wrist
turns on the AC full blast at 7 in the morning
don't forget the orchids, water with ice cubes
twice a week at most
masturbates in the shower
twice a week at least
102° San Joaquin valley heat
rewriting the recipe for vichyssoise
in a feverish lull of couch-induced slumber
hummingbirds in the hydrangeas
mated ducks in the swimming pool
and skunks scouting eggs
at dusk too beleaguered to frequent the taco truck
parked in the Union 66 gas station parking lot
picks up the mail every other day
all the modern conveniences
even the pets are robotic
expected to narrate the sports section and comics
don't forget to collect grandma at the airport
scouring the toilet bowl with antiseptic musings
free to strut about the waxed floorboards naked
3 am dancehall mannequin animation
every inhabitant of the world ignorant
of His Majesty's pristine velvet finery
oh and don't forget to launder the bedding
you maudlin hobo you

THE VETERAN

I switched to cigars
After smoking cigarettes for 30 years

I switched to vodka
After drinking bourbon for 30 years

I switched to Asian women
After fucking white girls for 30 years

The penalties are killing me

FEATHER AND BONE

quit chicken,
chews like rubber, or
manna in reverse.

new corpses sprayed
with pesticides, a fresh form
of cannibalism.

how was it that once, bathed in milk?
with the low chanting,
the incense burning,

and finally,
the token ritual
sacrifice.

I purchase my
flesh from
the organic market.

romantic life reduced to
gimme this,
gimme that,

coveting the password
for that
pirated porn site.

WHAT'S A BLACKOUT BETWEEN FRIENDS

did I mention
I had another episode?
like that time when I woke up
in a 6 am taxicab
with just my pants on
and a thin cotton blanket
freshly delivered from the ER
at Swedish Hospital.

strangest of cities,
this time
shackled to the gurney, like
a mental patient. disconcerting
to know that why
I even left the apartment at all
was simply for a hot bowl of beef
pho.

did I mention?
just for the record,
I have ridden several species of animals;
a bunch of horses,
a burro,
a camel in the Negev,
and an elephant
at Marine World Africa USA.

a man can only carry himself so far.

DINNERTIME

I thought
basil pesto fettuccine
steamed asparagus
heirloom tomato

Nothing
is the right size anymore
bent on character assassination
it's impossible to fit in

A bright advertisement
for petty theft

A salt shaker
laced with white rice
stolen from the corner taco joint

Ice in a pint glass and a Stoli shot
a marijuana cigarette laced with
strychnine

Because jerking off
is contrite
in the face of a news age
where saga is fake news fodder.

NIGHTMARE REENACTMENT

I was walking along with my best friend's sister
along the patchily paved streets of downtown San Francisco
just holding hands and occasionally cooing
closing in on the vicinity of my wretched abode
maybe getting ready for you-know-what
despite evidence on the wall above the bed
of numerous smeared cockroach killings
that's when suddenly, out of the sky
a black and heavy military-looking aircraft
came barreling in overhead way too low for comfort
I looked up at it
and said
According to recent entries in my dream journal
that fucker is going down
and then the thing flew straight into the BofA building
and burst into flames
as the monolithic structure collapsed
of course chaos ensued
chaos, chaos with a capital C
while all I could think was
Goddamnit, talk about spoiling the moment

DEATH OF AN AMERICAN POET

first I flew to Paris
then I subscribed to Netflix

I'M ICING MY ANKLE

after tripping and falling out of the bus
after a 30-day stint in County jail
where fresh air is breathed and exercise performed
once a week for an hour in a cavernous concrete room
with a worn-out basketball
and a rusty rim lacking a net.

I'M ICING MY WRIST

while at the same time
evincing southpaw longhand
how to flip an egg or
jerk off
with my
newly discovered
left hand
light a Bic lighter
wipe my ass
put on socks
eye a keyhole
stir a damn drink

with my left hand
newly unearthed

CHRISTMAS MORNING

Not too smart
I captured
a mouse with
wings
shaped like ears
    feeding
    Quivering
at twatty tweets

it's so close to where
I live
that neon
Blinking through the
fog
Replacing dreams with equity

a very convenient zipper
installed
    butcher boots, tight corsets
    and bottles of ammonia in the pantry
The feral
mastectomy
Not too damn negligible

Life unframed and simmering
    in a pot
Dump in all the remains
of the hunt
of the contents of the garbage bag

the ends of onions and carrots
    leeks
Mirepoix of the dust of some pregnant colossus

I can see you smiling
I wish I could punch like Joe Fraser or Ali
    through a forest of seaweed
As the newborns
    whimper and squeal

As a cockroach is trapped, legs caught in wet
paint
Newly applied

The crows caw on Christmas morning
Since that's what
I'm up to these days
Since that's what we're all
up against

There is service
definitely!
delivery service
Online delivery

Where you better
tip 'em good
You got to tip 'em
especially that fine-ass
Alissa
    An ebony beauty
    although, doubtlessly, she would not hesitate

for a second
To steal my identity

I hobble about re-injuring my wound
Gotta get thoughtful
Try to avoid getting black out drunk
Useful, avoid
  diarrhea and the
  stink of broken veins

I wear 2 shirts against the aroma and
resort to crutches, while birdsong is
Meekly ingrained against
the window

I could use some
steroids
a series
of quality medications
Or just a good hit off the streets

Them little critters miming in the dark
Invincible
You crush them and out comes protein
  in a smear of innocence
  I'd like some sleep
not like broken hair and bad skin
but dreamless

I forgot about
the raindrop denying fishbowl effervescence

La la, la la la
De da

I forgot the return
That I flew into de Gaulle for a song
mussels in the cafes
sunlight glitter strobe off the Seine
        and when the snow came
        We were all trapped

finally and
Brilliantly

HEAD SHOT

the beak
longer
lips thinner

yet
still armed
with acidic wit

gaze somewhat
cataract-white

earlobes pickled in
pink

brain waves
reduced
to spheres of carbon

some
crystallized trinket
stashed from infancy
for protection.

PARADISICAL

I fell out of last year
like spoiled lettuce
off a rattletrap flatbed
only to lie to the minor masses
in the manner of
modern promises

falling out of that
satellite from space
an obsolete
splash-landing
I haven't done laundry
for about 2 weeks

even my notebooks
smell a bit musty
the old ballpoint
loyal to the letter
New Year's Eve like a
frayed trampoline

as I reach the heights
adjectives stew in media
like a chippy
nuclear exchange
just another day
on the books

LOVE POEM

there's a race, a celebration
every time we wake up
still breathing

the sun against the wall
like a curse
on anybody else

but damn, you never looked
hotter
in those Ray Bans

I SPENT THE OTHER DAY

laid out like a corpse
because a turn of fabrication
elevated an injury into a reality

then she said
Sign this.

I couldn't tell what
the weather outside was like
but it sure wasn't spring

driftwood prosecuting ocean waves
with the gulls screaming
out of frame

then she said
I need to see some identification.

I borrowed time from
a seascape I saw
imprisoned behind the plate glass window
of the thrift store

then she said, pointing her pen
And I'll need your initials here.

it was a dream
where I rode a horse
in full gallop

leaning forward
oceanside wind on my face

that's how I spent the other day
like an overdrawn bank account

DIFFERENCES IN SALARY

it's hard to breathe
then add the sirens
then the News disclosure
    blaming all the wrong people

the window fan, plugged into the wall, wheezing.

what I need is
    an unbiased haircut.

I get tired fast
especially after 2 slices
    of custom-designed pizza.

insulted 8 hours straight by any old
    karmic host,
or a tightly wrapped cigar
imported,
    La Republica Dominicana.

I was certainly not
    the little-league talent they expected.

RHYMES WITH FUCK IT

Bag o' bones
Bag o' bongs

Los pistoles
No amigos

Custom fit
Fucking shit

Who needs Pablo
She got a dildo

My soul blacker
Than a weed-whacker

GRAVITY

at least something works

NOCTURNE

theres's a point every minute, each second
where outside our hovels
the trees
mimic our lives
swaying unconsciously with the wind.

but upstairs
I got problems
electricity shorted out
all efforts to survive
consolidated
into a pocket flashlight.

never mind the smart phone, somebody'll
eventually cancel that.

naturally, I'm as immortal as…

damn,
I gotta take a piss

A NEW SCENARIO

I listened to the radio all morning
Just sports talk for me
No more jazz or classical
I'm funny
I've changed with the passing years
So I went out and bought a can of tuna
With basketball stats on my mind
Win or lose
I use rigatoni to further my addiction to canned fish
Some olive oil and black pepper
Why not
My foot is swollen due to recurrent nightmares
Falling out of bed
Falling in love with women
At the bus stop
I use a Bic pen to sketch out my future
It's a grimly pretty portrait
Riddled with gunfire
On the bricks at Civic Center
Because I no longer attend classes in ethics
Despite imaginary parole
It's the shits
Mythology caught up with pathos
Can't explain the sealed jar of peanut butter
Lonely on the shelf for months
Ever since I gave up processed sugar
Ever since I painted black acrylic over the mirror
Ever since the blithe sobriety of uselessness overwhelmed me
And now a soundtrack of liquidated food porn

With gold leaf embossing
A hate poem
A death poem
Perhaps 35% of what I heard on the radio today
All the advertisements for
The usual industries
Lawyers, casinos, diamonds, divorce
Where to dispose of your car or truck or property
The type of jingle worse than constipation
Why not
Win or lose
Your next Scratch ticket
Your next fantasy
Rain and rot and ruin
Ensues
Yet outside the window
A new scenario
Total stillness as sunlight flirts with the leaves
Transforming chlorophyll into infinity

THE ACCIDENT

nearing the last exit he swerved left,
lights bright in his eyes
into traffic but first;
he borrowed the car from his sister-in-law
who owed him money.

good money,
the kind that bails you out or
proposes marriage.

it was a bad night,
he lost a bundle
on a wrong pick, and not much time left
to pare the fingernails.

the coughing was getting worse,
the subscription to losses
weekly,
then the inquiry,
followed by a less than discerning
investigation, the kind that squares you
on the map.

while cold waves crash
on every planet in the caravan
unattended.

hard candy, cashing out, dipping for apples in
zero gravity.

MANUAL FOR REINCARNATION

until you've been so drunk
you end up curled up in a shopping cart
slobbering in fetal position at dawn in a parking lot

until you've murdered an unsuspecting cockroach
or a fly against the windowsill
rather than your worst enemy

until you've drunk vodka shots
then frothy beer backs with the full moon
perched on your shoulders

good old Luna serving as executioner
because under all that weight
you might as well just take a dirt nap

4TH OF JULY PERVERSION

so the dogs are really
pissed off
they're barking at the top
of their lungs, while
meanwhile
that hot blonde lady
down the hall
just turned
30.

she informed me of this as we
met in the elevator
going down
to the lobby.
she's originally from Marin County
and is living
with a minor
Chechen gangster
who is currently driving
an Uber
between assassinations.

I get by because I
fantasize
about licking her armpits.
oh yeah
and her tight little purple asshole too.

ACCESS

in the old days we
watched stuff like
demolition derby
Creature Features
Saturday morning cartoons
and all day
Sunday
pro football
on one of 3
TV networks
not including PBS.

we looked forward to it,
even armed with the first video game:
Pong.

if you liked tennis,
Pong was the
antithesis.

back then we used to
amuse ourselves
in various ways:
peanut butter and marmalade
spread on a raw
matzah,
or jerking off to that famous
Farrah Fawcett
swimsuit poster.

nowadays you can watch
anything you want
anywhere
at any time.

you can witness
any kind of exploitative
Homo sapiens
coupling,
or a colorized
WWII
military coup,
or a terrorist cell
beheading,
or perhaps
a faulty satellite
disabled and falling,
headed
to your next

vacation destination.

THE MONGREL

for all the times I curse
or entertain impure thoughts
I verily explain to God:
it's a dog's life
You've given me
and certainly not
pedigreed

BACK TO BLACK AND WHITE

hermit crabs scuttle across pearl moonscapes
while the mice in the floorboards
have their own brand of justice

I gotta go to the doctor
because something is wrong
even the butcher shop's closed

waves pulse and recede, frothy white
thoroughbred horses breathe heavily
trapped in their ancient skulls
while the sky just storms and rains

you might be a break in the monotony
a saxophonist encouraging call and response
then you quit smoking for good
while I notice
in the middle of the night
a pair of scissors at my throat

who listens to forewarnings?
just follow the fireworks
and not so suddenly
the ceiling fan ceases to rotate

electricity down
of course the water is shut off without any notice
it takes very little panic before

the people start flocking for the toilets
for more reasons than one

but no way to boil out the salt
the acidity
the shit

a grey sheen decolorizes reality
the film strip of life finally achieving the circuitous
evolution of art

6 SHOT, SIDE ELYSIAN

hot for a change at Golden Gardens
the fire pit roasting aria of schooners
on the southern side of the street
cool air-conditioned poison lounge at Golden City
Dragon Lady sloshing around the navel
painted on the smoke a riverboat jamboree
juke wailing Dance with me, twirl
a girl around pinky cowboy muzzle

fireworks define fatherhood of nations
slaughtering daily blessings at breakfast
dreams at a premium, bowl cracked hibiscus
blue with need she's emergent from liquid forest
licking wounds, lost but for the stripes
impaled upon handheld bayonets
zebra in medical scrubs

sparks descend from on high
progeny of stars

for the traffic lights and aluminum
squeal of insecticide

POSTCARD FROM OVERSEAS

2 French cats
one black, one white,
have gone missing

there's a flyer
taped to the light pole
in a distinctive foreign tongue

oui oui,
pussy,
meow

how would that
sound
retrospective of death?

I myself have vanished
as well,
been gone for a good couple months

nobody I know has
noticed-
oui oui oui

all the
way
home

FREEDOM FLIER

in the air
plummeting
through clouds like wet
tissue paper
some say a fall
others insist a push
canyon engulfed
sun like knife flint
of cold gleam
within, within
his skin resists beneath
space suit lined with badger pelt
water broken off granite mirrors
bridge blown to bits
train hurtling after
shadow puppet intertwined
outside campfire
crackling
shadows fleeing
small children holding ears in hands
for bruised dreams to follow
what once embodied air and sunshine
hawks and a briefly tremulous whine
of miscalculated weaponry
dusk on the battlefield
questioning why
anybody would jump out of a perfectly good airplane

TEXT ME IN THE SKY

limp pizza
expired haiku

text me
in the sky

after I expire
blood smeared

on the towel
mind the eyes

slinky blindfold
it's your call

WE AS A PEOPLE

the other night yet another local city burned
I can smell it in the walls
it's becoming normalized in California
to absorb the Inferno
to don customized gas masks
as the walls of everywhere
teem with vermin
I wish I had a dog
to alert me of these ideas
or a Sigmund Freud bobblehead
the last couple weeks have killed dozens of people
in California
as science maintains
we as a people
have certain enemies in high places

END OF IT

there'll be no time
for us that recognize
the passing of it
to remember

Michelangelo, Mozart, Rembrandt
imagery dashed to the depths
pianos blown out of the sky

and what about
institutionalized wet brains
robotically chewing some factory processed carrion

what we are
there will be no time
left to describe

the fury evolved
in the evolution of
failure

it's a damn shame
I was planning on a starlet
on each elbow
by age 60

NEEDS

I need sex
I need speed
I need booze
I need sleep
I need dreams

sushi delivery
wouldn't hurt either

WATCHING A CON IN ACTION

is better than noir
is better than popcorn at the porn site
as the old men shuffle around the dive bars
allowing the young vixens to fleece them
it's about time and place
and a nice retirement package
a tidy divorce
a dependable drinking problem
the girl swirling about the bar is working
the old men and it's systematic
some foreign tourists loiter around at the entrance
but ultimately decide
that this scene is a bit out of their depth
and yet
it is not
and cannot
borderline the original subterranean
transaction
all in all it gives me the creeps
I'm just waiting
for something substantial to happen
in the wrong place at the worst time
with benign
sotto voce
fluttering in my ears like fireflies

THE GARDEN OF EDEN

we start out like
hourglasses

and end up as
fire hydrants

VESSELS

we know so little
yet brag about
explain about
nod and shake hands over
the infinitesimal
the clairvoyant
the absolute
very little
or too much
one grocery item
over another
one billboard
that new product
the next election
a clever commercial
but what about
the eyes of the spider
the loins of statues
those flashes of insight
a sonnet memorized
the square root
of intuition
we are so full
of so very little
it is positively
breathtaking

I KNOW EVIL WHEN I SEE IT

it's the details that give you away
as a saint
or a fraud
or inevitably
as an assassin
the arabesques drawn in the air
a volley of gunfire,
a vault of missiles
or finally
by the painter's touch
say
back in the Renaissance
when people bled pigs
in cobblestoned
alleyways
while children wept
before being sold off for
prostitution or
slavery
whatever's handiest
as the cherry trees and olive
branches thrive
in full
blossom

NOT TOO KEEN ON FURTHERING MY EDUCATION

I wheeze a little
left eye a bit blurred
I recognize about 13% of the flowers
while bearing witness
to the utter decline of humanity

dying to know the whys and wherefores?
pregnant with beans and carne asada
the albino ape
blessed with a 25K
word vocabulary

THE BANDWAGON

let's just hurry up already
and give the planet back to the forces
of nature
to the grizzlies and blue whales
to the daffodils and honeybees
I'm sick of dying
and drinking water out of plastic bottles
even my shoes are degraded
let's just close up shop

I remember my old man telling me
if you like 'em get two pairs
while he was talking about shoes
I myself
worried about the red button
AIDS
and the wart on the toe of my girlfriend
it's time and time again
to revoke faith in
favor of dying

if you want cheering up
don't come to me
there's a W A N T E D poster
for humanity
some little green men
or worse
the Secret Service
and who gets paid in the end?

those with total lack of empathy

RULES TO THE GAME

there are rules to the
game
I must embrace them
at all times
which is
why I'm not dead and buried

I have certain role models

her name is Selena
or Miley
or Scarlett
as long as her voice
is low and
throaty

okay
I get it
if they had blinded me
as an infant
broke my legs
offered me crutches
or better yet
a wheelchair

a $200 pass in a game of
Monopoly
I'd be better off

maybe
I should quit watching
movies
and absorbing
social media
forever

I sleep late
into the afternoon
for a reason

despite the
jackhammers
and petrol in the air
staining my curtains

one more trip to
the library
can't hurt
but it does

I learn more and benefit
how's that change my
game?

book read and a penchant
for cutlery

FIRST THINGS FIRST

so whatever it is
it's gigantic
and getting
closer
and in the middle of the night
3 or 4 in the aye-em
or whatever
it's called
when the moon decides
on it's own
to judge the human
species

when it's
a call to
action

it's the utility trucks
the recycling trucks
the garbage trucks

it's special ops
black ops
they've found out
I hate them
since the plans that I
made
under the scrutiny

of dreaming
are abstruse.

I am always
in pain
because I get
so drunk
so I can sleep
through the noisy
nonsensical
palliative of dawn

first
the veil of vodka
then
in the morning
I call someone
to say I'm
unavailable
or otherwise
injure myself

how's that
for a laugh
any old guy who'd
pilfer your
girlfriend
with a cigar behind his ear
and a Cadillac limo
parked, engine running,
in front
of the bar
ought to know better

first things first
let's stick with
haven't I met you
once before?

THERE IS ONLY ONE COLOR

put your finger in it
like a shark-toothed gingerbread house
get out on the street
despite the conspicuous absence
of French Symbolist poets
plant a seed,
quit buying crap you don't need
chant: one plate, one fork, one cup, one spoon
give the rest away, gratis
surrender your wants
to the impoverished indigence
use a laser beam to cut squares from the sky
to let down the stars, to lay waste
to the hive-like inhuman consciousness
bent on ensnaring, enslaving
the free spirit of creative forces,
to shatter and shove black reptilian oaths
vowed in penthouse palaces
back up their vile asses
take it back
channel the anarchy born of the free womb
there is only one color
hotly coursing beneath the skin
uniting us all
it is wine, the chianti of love
it is blood
it is ours

THE DAUBER

You don't want to know about
the remnants hanging on
the wall. They are the result
of failed *pinging* experiment. I say
fail because the computer
recognized *painting* as
pinging. Which makes more sense
than the body breaking down
and demanding mental facility
to overwhelm lack of
mobility. In other words,
I could sure use a wheelchair.

LE TEMPS PRESSE

all I have left
of my old man's belongings
is a black woven leather belt
and something short of an inheritance
that's quickly dwindling

I've lost weight so the
belt's getting tighter and tighter

kinda like a noose

THE CITY

A spring day
Cherry blossoms like dabs of cream
Against the chill blue sky
The Panhandle
Vibrant with green grass
Birds cavorting in the shade of eucalyptus trees

A nature poem
Plopped
In the middle of the City
Which for the most part
Is a soulless reservoir of filth
I guess the point is I did give it a try
Probably need a middle finger removed
As well as a liver
For toasting to the gods
For 40 years
My span of life on the planet

It's the infection of wisdom
Allowing me to totally shut out
All my family and friends

I listen to sports commentary on the radio
As if we're old friends
It works for me

How about an avocado and a couple apples
From the grocery store up the street 3 blocks away

Back on arrival my feet throbbing
3 ibuprofen later
Need I mention asthma
A fierce need to do laundry?

Meanwhile the gas guzzlers roll by in the street
Staining my curtains
My lungs

And the discipline
I held dear
When I once was an artist

WHAT HAPPENS

what happens to your shoes
when you die

what happens to the moon
maybe it turns blood red

or doesn't show up at all
since it's raining so hard

I NEED A SHOWER

and a shave
I believe in ghosts
and aliens
everybody I've loved in fiery embraces
is dead
or will die someday
hungry
sleepy
I need to do laundry
and catch up on my reading
but my left eye has cataracts
while my right eye is fixated on the sun
there's a possum in the basement
and somewhere, maybe everywhere
paint is drying
I dream in color
and the stop-action is vicarious
there's always a new movie to watch
or an oil spill
or the daily presidential malfunction
I like coconut oil
but during this heat wave
June of this year

it's melted to liquid
but more than
anything
I could use a shower
a clean towel
a window open
the zephyr quickening
I crack my knuckles
and boys?
why not
another shot

COUNTRY TOWN CITY SELF

In the zing of mosquito wings
The terrible periphery
Inherent in all things

I walk the road
Ease on my mind
Pain in every joint

Elephant or wicked ant
Man fearing mouse
Sycophant

Ever more than ever
I wake to small
Terror

In the saxophone of pretty
Things
Blows a natural ring

Bringing me all back
To the original
Black loving heart

All starts begin with
And end
Bitching at

TEMPERATURE VS CLIMATE

what feels good is a cool breeze
from an otherwise unsuspecting nuclear window

I got some time left
despite the neon enforced affliction

there is that truth
when the appetite is sated with steamed eggs or a mango

I got a minute to contemplate lifetimes, not yours
but mine

and a broad erasure mechanism
to blot it all from existence

the door is cracked open
so they can look in on what is left of me

it feels good, that breeze from the outside
working its way in

I know I'm meaningless
a dab in the spacetime continuum with obsolete specs

there is that truth
how many languages does it take to interpret

what is mine, is yours, is
ours.

WHAT STINKS

my style is pinkish
in the old
pink sink,

so when I puke in it
the lights come on and
everything seems resplendent.

how else to dye porcelain?
or manage lipstick, a broken
skull

or your first girlfriend
or your last
look in the mirror.

my memories stained
with spent
erections.

a history of suspect associations
plus
I broke my glasses again.

in the endgame it's a little sad
that I'd rather
watch some porn

than sit up nights
playing Scrabble
with you.

SUNRISE COMES WITH ITS OWN SET OF RULES

rats can fly
believe it
I've seen it
infestation is no laughing matter
every day another threat
from the TV screen
from the Orange President
no wonder nothing rhymes with Orange
or the White House Press Secretary
or that punk pre-pubescent plagiaristic Neo-Nazi
writing the speeches
rats not only fly
but burrow deeply into the American subconscious
and wheel and canter into the dream
don't you get it?
the flowers of resistance are being subjugated
to swarms of reverse remarks
it's an eclipse damn it!
sunrise comes with yet another verbal attack
against Americans
Congresswomen!
female Americans I want to be good friends with
that I want a family with
of color
of freedom
of solidarity
on the West lawn
or is it the East
or is it the
last

DOWN THE HALL

"It can be a natural, zesty enterprise" -Maude Lebowski

I was taking out the trash
down the hall
when I heard
from behind door #416
the hump of bedsprings and moans of pleasure.

good God, I thought,
it's Thumper getting fucked.

I call her Thumper
because when she clomps down the hall
you can hear it a mile away
each footstep an explosion of puissance.

she's a young,
rather thick woman
her cell phone attached to her ear
like an enormous leech
in the elevator or
waiting for an Uber on the sidewalk outside the hotel
leaves falling dumbly
from the trees.

myself, I notice the floating,
skittering leaves
and the small birds at 6 am
while my bed has been empty for years

just how I've grown to
like it.

still, it's nostalgic to recall
the times I used to
fuck the women
without a care in the world
making the bedsprings sing
and for that memory
I thank
dear Thumper
in room #416.

I hope you got off.

I WANT TO FALL ASLEEP

without biting off my tongue
a glass of cold creek water on the nightstand
clouds careening in my mind
looking forward to bad haircuts
legendary hangovers and indecipherable quotes
I want to simulate a golden eagle
a hibernating grizzly
paint being applied to a masterpiece
bartending anonymously somewhere in the Caribbean
bagging groceries in Brooklyn
scouting for the Apocalypse
"Death is most definitely a
5-tool prospect, while Famine
couldn't hit a curve in slow motion"

THE CYCLE

like the serpent
I was born to
in the Chinese zodiac
I am shedding skin
and hardening,
curving into an
antique arabesque
older than wrought iron
set into the gates
of someplace exalted,
otherworldly
and patently
a scam on the face
of space-time.

it's not my fault
that every 12 years
another generation
is born, like myself
riddled with innuendo
and the compulsive
urge to self-destruct,
like curses graffitied
to the palace walls,
jackhammers taken
to marble Pietas
following the one
rule of the game:
nothing at all.

IN THE HOSPITAL ROOM

you keep wondering
if the footsteps
are coming for you
to tell you either everything's gonna be peachy
or you're a basket case
after all the battles
the voices in the hall
random people in agony
riding on the gurney was not amusing
such white walls
the concerned smiles on the nurses
for the newly practically interred invalid
and the x-ray room like out of science fiction
in the fluorescent light
of the hospital room
my skin looks like a lobster's
scaly red exoskeleton
I listen to the footsteps
almost hoping for the worst
let's get this shit-show on the road
I always liked to travel
lost and found in a foreign clime
a beach
an orchard
an orchid
some broken down 3rd world hotel room
with a bottle and a fix on the side table
lying on a gurney
my back itches

eyes blinded by strobe
degrading in contrast to spring blooming outside
the TV broken
in the hospital room
where I never thought I'd end up
I used to fly
when I was a kid
they called me Bird
now I must use my mind
to paint pictures
chicken feet streaking the windows
like tears of God

NOW IT'S JUST YOU AND ME

Stop
The message isn't getting through
There was this morning
Parallel to birdsong
Endquote
It was nightbirds
It was crows
Quit it
It was the faint cries of carrion birds circling
I have to admit
Watching the CCVC
In my next life
You bought my contract
On some black site
Once
To see me again
Knowing
I would've given myself away for free
If I'd've known to forfeit
The eagle
Or the seashore seagull
Stop
All I do
Is pick out the chum
Arrange over-the-counter meds
Since I'm required reading
In the books
In the shops
Quote

It was mosquitoes, finally
Or sharks
Excess dream and cold sweats
That woke me from a particular reverie
My team that
Won the World Series a very
Long time ago
Stop

SHORT ORDER THEORY OF EVOLUTION

the first step
is the hardest
there's a lot of
wobbling going on
you haven't even
uttered a single word
life is a warm tit
cries punctuated
with smiles
sleep in snatches
running the parents
dog-tired ragged
the second step
is assimilation
into the human
and societal world
it takes years
it takes decades
centuries
and you never quite
get it right
especially when armed
to the teeth and
seething with rage
jazz may soothe or
maybe a couple shots
and a mindless smoke
a nice girl with

a toned body
but taken for granted
these little pleasures
are nothing compared
to venting a soul's
worth of passion for
innuendo and shameless
thirst for power
the last step
is ordering munitions
off the internet
freely and anonymously
the protection of
the 2nd Amendment
hanging like unwashed laundry
over your head
sure to mold
perfectly in time
to your warped
sense of entitlement
there's a wheelchair
for all of you
psychotic killers
you never interpreted
the first step as a
positive
I'm sorry your parents
or whoever abused you
survived beyond puberty
meanwhile the twinkle in the eye
the cuteness and
birthday
pinatas go to
waste

RUN FOR IT

Duchamp knew the score
with his piece of string
unstrung on the wall
of his post-war apartment
in the heart of New York City
not to mention the chess set
and the French lessons
and whoops!
quitting art
far as we knew

I would like to play
chess with a naked woman
I would even play checkers,
or go fish

having to rely
on an inheritance
has somewhat stymied my creative approach

so I look to the past
and those sullen pioneers of conception
say Darwin, or Vivaldi
a few others I can't recall

and what about all those
friends I avoid like sandpaper
in real-time

even though occasionally they bring me
tacos
and acrylics they can't use anymore

so I've been
painting on towels pilfered
from the hotel
the management doesn't seem to mind
as long as
rent is on time

I'm hoping to
subsidize
my lack of imagination
with quilted hues
from the magic brush

you know the one,
where you just escape death
by a hair's breath
that breath you take after
missing the last bus

THE SPOILS

now more than ever
I get a talking-to
from the dreams

it's my parents or siblings
old friends long ago passed
they want the truth, verdad, pravda
I lay into them
since I'm angry and terrified

I have the stomach of 6 cows
I need a distraction!
music, sports…
but the radio spreads virus
and according to the myriad TV networks
anything is possible
sci-fi, zombies, rom-coms…
meaning, inevitably
we are
all going
to die

but will it be
beautiful
like butterflies
after chrysalis

odds always favor the house

AWOL

it was supposed to be
me reclining easily
all up there in Heaven
surrounded by hot barmaids in bikinis
and clear blue Hawaiian shorelines
fruity drinks, whole barbecued pigs,
an opiated dream.

but when they discovered that
I don't use punctation much
they took me by force
handcuffed and muffled
the balaclava stripped off
my white ass and shoved into my mouth.

what a bunch of assholes
they took selfies with my body as well
"We caught the fucking pervert"
someone call the taxidermist.

PET STORY

I was in Harlem, I was in Havana
I walked my dog to a local cantina
and asked the staff quite politely
to kill, skin, and cook
my pet with sauce picante

we never got along that well
according to my allergies
plus the incessant yapping,
and that bitch down the hall
constantly complaining
about the noise

I'll give you noise
try stuffing a bloody tampon
in your ear, or better yet
a thousand used condoms

BORN AGAIN VEGETARIAN

I want to say something
about the pork chop
seasoned with salt and cayenne

flat on a plate
waiting to be fried,
faceless as an atom bomb

and certainly not kosher
verboten in my sister's house
poor poor piggy

you died for nothing
because I am too drunk to cook
your dumb ass

I'd rather daydream, while waiting
for it to finally rain
after too many months of

hallucinatory ennui
for fuck sakes!
the *cucarachas* can have you.

IF WE'RE LUCKY

Sorry to complain yet again, but
I should write a book about it:
"The Cockroach Chronicles".
I must know more about these tiny militaristic beasts
Than any of my fellow women or man.
These creatures are obviously conspiring a revolution
Here in my little room;
They are fast as fuck as I descend with the killing thumb.
They even know how to leap for their lives,
Off the walls, off cooking utensils, even out of my drinking glass,
And yet
With a practiced swat with a magazine or a stained shirt
They're history.
Well, at least one of them.
But the annoying bastards, there's an endless supply of them;
They keep me up nights, haunting.
I ought to write a book. And sell it.
Money is what I need to make.
The problem is I have absolutely zero interest in researching
Mother fucking cockroaches.
I have arthritis,
Plus some stricken thing I know nothing about, residing sibilantly
In my bones.
There's this horrible damning surge on my skin,
And every time I watch a new sitcom
I depend on a new insectile murder to think,
Something based on science.
While all the while I represent the oasis
For my noncompliant friends.

They roam around in the dark spaces of my room,
Especially in the drawers,
Where I keep my boxers and socks,
Where it's dark
Just how I like it, by reflection, myself.
It's hard to be at war with a mirror image, your twin.
Ask Kafka, he wrote about waking up in bed, transformed.
Look where it got him.
My roaches are a lot smaller; it's easier to kill them.
I heard or read somewhere that cockroaches
Are not good for people with asthma.
Those little exoskeletal bastards.
They steal my water,
They organize in the drawers,
They build armies in the closet,
Soon they'll inhabit the moon, or maybe Venus.
Try to terraform that scenario.

GOD

some kind savior
who I don't know
left one of those mini-watermelons
on the long table
in the lobby.

I grabbed that sucker and ran.

a fine summertime treat, the size
of a soccer ball.
and for free.

I don't hang out in the lobby much
except
for access to the ice machine.

I enjoy my ice.

first I broke my hand,
then I broke my fist.

I've also been left pizza,
all the while
totally ignoring
the birds outside in the
trees.

it's not my fault or my
whim.

some kind body
comes to me in dreams.

sometimes she's a
geisha,
other times a ballerina,
a black belt,
a Joan of Arc.
whoever she is
she reflects
the very first time I lit that
bonfire

out there beyond the cosmos.

THE CROWS

this could be my last utterance
that's what the crows insist
jawing outside my window
over the city street.

crows, they live longer than you think
reservoirs of intelligence
camping in the rain gutters
even though it hasn't rained for months.

my last breath
like a silhouette aflame,
or the last downpour
ever to make asphalt sing.

this could be my final love
or laughter,
my last longing
or craving for revenge.

the crows bring me
sparkly trinkets
because I feed them bread crumbs
on a regular basis.

CLEMENT STREET

Lucy had hair on her wiggly toes;
it was obvious since she was perched up high
half naked atop the refrigerator.

We were drinking because
I'd finally caught up on the rent;
celebrating, like beasts after the kill.

Lucy played the harp or at least she had one-
she was also studying film.
the air in her bedroom, fetid at best.

Adrienne slept in the room right off the kitchen,
weeping into her hourglass of gin.
her boyfriend was a car mechanic.

I lucked into the room facing the street with all the good light.
I wrote a poem about Vincent van Gogh.
It was probably about 4 lines too short.

I wanted Lucy, though I ignored movies and was
4 lines into getting it on with Adrienne,
who panted for me to yank her hair and slap her ass.

San Francisco was different in those days.
I could cook up a failsafe design by satellite
just short of Seal Beach and dandelions.

3 THOUGHTS

The first hardcover book I ever bought new was
Death Poems of Japanese Poets
Back in 1985, it cost me 20 bucks

What I should do now is heat up those black beans
From Walgreens
Add raisins for no reason

I get why I'm finally
Gonna die
It's easier than shaving early in the morning

FREEDOM

elephant ears punctured by fish hooks;
I was born to survive,
wandering the familiarity of our language,
motivated by sleazy style.
the rain in the streets is the difference
the little shrimp and octopi from the sewers
we eat them, before sucking their skulls for flavor.
get real, I was born to
increase the animation of my hands;
but rest assured
I never boiled a man's head in a pot to avoid prosecution.
African dog on the prowl,
American coyote coldly seeking;
in China they manufacture your aural cacophony,
in India
elephants are rather scarce;
it would take an outfit like Barnum and Bailey's
to reinforce how I was honored to escape.

PAPER

people use paper
and rubber
without any idea
why the forest existed before us

got a flight planned?
where do you think those hot wheels came from
to ensure your safe landing
on United or Southwest or Virgin

I used to write on paper
I still do sometimes
when it's free, whoopee!
but you can't rely on
some tube of whitewashed newspaper,
exclusive to your ass

don't mess with the trees
they fight back
ever slowly, in a dimension you'll never see coming

PINK IS THE COLOR

I got a new phone
not the kind of phone like
back in the olden days when
you had to remember
the numbers

old black telephones you could
wield like weapons
telephones that rang incessantly
like in scores of 70s movies
or the jaws of a land shark

my old phone was lifted from a toilet stall
because I left it there by mistake
after doing my business and wiping my ass
which was as usual
on the line

for a couple hundred
the new phone seller claimed online
that the color
was "rose/gold"
sometimes it's not so bad being lied to

WHEN I THINK OF MUSIC

I think of Gustav Mahler
John Coltrane or the
Velvet Underground

but I don't think about music as much as I used to
back then I was blue and cold
standing stiff like a tree

back when I was
fraught
with conviction

nowadays, nice and quiet suffices
punctuated of course by the inevitable
sounds of the city

fire engines, trash trucks
police sirens, car alarms
and the occasional nocturnal scream

it's when I think of the why and what for
that's when the music
metastasizes

HOW MANY MOVIES

what I love about the
rain
is that it beats on the window like
the purity of your heart
the one that rules the universe
as you sleep
as I watch.

all I know is we
are warm and together.
but what do I really
know.

chemical processes,
karmic diversions
and suddenly
the radiator has
finally
issued demands.

the light switch with its infinite knowledge
remains uncertain.

it may be a hell of a storm,
but way short
of what's coming.